T0132333

PATRICIA LOUISE NEWNUM

Devon
in
Heaven

AuthorHouse™
1663 Liberty Drive
Bloomington, IN 47403
www.authorhouse.com
Phone: 1 (800) 839-8640

Published by AuthorHouse 04/26/2019

ISBN: 978-1-7283-0879-1 (hc)
ISBN: 978-1-7283-0843-2 (sc)
ISBN: 978-1-7283-0844-9 (e)

Scripture quotations marked KJV are from the Holy Bible, King James Version (Authorized Version). First published in 1611. Quoted from the KJV Classic Reference Bible, Copyright © 1983 by The Zondervan Corporation.

Print information available on the last page.

Any people depicted in stock imagery provided by Getty Images are models, and such images are being used for illustrative purposes only. Certain stock imagery © Getty Images.

This book is printed on acid-free paper.

authorHOUSE®

Devon in Heaven

I Corinthians 2:9 (KJV) .. Eye hath not seen, nor ear heard, neither hath entered into the heart of man, the things which God hath prepared for them that love Him.

Written by: Patricia Louise Newnum

This book is dedicated to:
Tyler- brother
Zachary- brother
Jessica- Mother
Sandi- Grandmother
April - Aunt

And all the family of Devon in Heaven.

*The scripture reference
from the King James
Version of the Bible
was suggested by
Ronald W. Newnum.*

He ran down the heavenly path in a flurry
To see the flowers bloom
For each one called his name out loud
And sang him a heavenly tune
He skipped down the street lined with
Diamonds and jewels
Then flew with the heavenly dove
Colors so bright added joy to light
And the sky was filled with such love
On his way through our kitchen past our heavenly cook
He grabbed morsels of heavenly bites
He exclaimed. "This is great"
Grabbed him a plate, then went off to play with his kite
The afternoon came, he lay down
To rest with his puppy next to his bed

The heavenly cloud that he snuggled into
Was so soft to this precious head
Oh My! He is happy – He dreams
Such sweet dreams of his
Mommy, his mamaw and more
He sighs a deep sigh, as he knows
That someday they will walk
Through the heavenly door
But until they arrive – He is more
Then alive – with his fun, games and joy
Be assured he is held in the arms of our Lord
And will always be your little boy
You really would not believe, Mommy
What it's like in Heaven
It started with a loving voice that called
Come here little Devon

This wonderful man named Jesus
Picked me up and carried me
To a safe home with God
And a beautiful living tree
He sat me in the branches and said,
Devon look around, see the joy,
Feel the caress and hear the happy sound.
The angels are gracious people with smiles
And laughter and fun.
They welcome everybody
When their time on Earth is done.

There's lots to do up here Mommy
I feed the lions and lambs and I am always
Talking to the Father and holding His hand.
I show Him all my money, and
I give Him some gum.
He says He always loves His
kids best because we're
Bright as the sun.

I climb the hills and cross the lake and build
Castles out of sand.
I am never lonely cause I'm with
The Great I Am
I have to say I miss you
But I never worry or fear
Because I know that someday you will also be here.

Till then, I Love You mommy,
Please be brave,
Your little boy Devon is not in the grave

Mamma sweet mamma, did you know what?
I am such a big boy now, I'm growing up
I can reach the second limb on God's living tree,
And I can make a sand hill higher than you and me
I can climb the highest mountain, swim a raging sea,
Tell my big brother, Tyler, that he'd be proud of me
I'm in Kindergarten now, I know how to count,
I can read, I can spell, and talk a great amount.
The angel teacher likes to hear answers that we say,
But asking questions seems to make him frown a certain way
How do we catch a moonbeam, and what makes it glow?
Is rain when God is crying, and is clouds made out of snow?
How come the snow is cold, and why are streets gold?
Tell me, tell me quick, I've really got to know.
Why are pearly gates made of pearls,
And why are we boys, and why are you a girl?
Why does doves coo, and why do lions roar?
How come we call Jesus Heaven's only door?

Dearest Mammy, Mamaw, and more, guess what
We went fishing on heaven's shore.
I caught a frog; we had some fun, Jesus fished too
'Cause His work is all done.
We ran up and down the heavenly hills.
We rode a horse on the heavenly trails.
We camped out on the heavenly ground.
You will never believe all the treasures we found
Not diamonds or pearls or silver or gold,
Some things new and some things old.
God says the treasure is stored for all time,
Will never get rusty or rot on the vine
We need not sell or pack away, it's there forever the angels say
It's the kind of laughter sent up by a child
Or good deeds that were done by the meek and mild,
Encouraging help of a wise old man
Or an uplifting spirit and an outstretched hand,

Henry's my buddy; he's tall you see.
In heaven, there's lots more kids like me.
We all have grandpas and grandmas who bless.
They are smarter than all the rest.
They fuss over us and such; and we go back for more,
And dozens of cousins come in through the door.

I hid my marbles way deep in a cave.
Mamaw, you'd be happy to see me behave.
I climbed in and got them and shared with the rest.
My manners were the very best.

Bubby, there's lots of things here to do.
We even have our own animal zoo.
No need to cage them, the monkeys and bears,
Elephants and tigers, and old grey mares.
Even the lion lies down with the lamb.
They like to stay close to the Great 'I Am'.

That's why Jesus died on the cross,
Took upon Him the sins of the lost,
Paid the price, the penalty, offered up so we can be free
Holy Spirit makes it happen, we are born again,
Truly a birth that will never end.
Just say. "I need You; I'm bad, You see,
But You can make me what you want me to be.
It's easy for kids. We know we do wrong,
So it's not hard to ask, that we can belong.
But sometimes a grown-up finds it hard to say
"Forgive me, Father, help me find Your Way."
So Great "I Am" provides, the Jesus Sacrifice,
Holy Spirit makes it true, the work is done for you.
My guardian angel is here to play, so I
must talk to you another day
His Name is so pretty; His wings just shine.
He has been with me from beginning of time.
I will live for all eternity, I will always love you, my sweet family.

ABOUT THE AUTHOR

Patricia Louise Newnum, commonly referred to as Patti, was born as Patricia Louise Kelley in Indianapolis, Indiana on January 27, 1942. Patti has indicated she had a happy childhood living in and around the city. Her memories included living near Brookville Road and Post Road where her mother and step-dad ran a small filling station. One of her fondest memories there included where she said, "I slept behind the candy counter."

Later, as Patti approached her mid-teens, she decided she was going to be married to Alvin Pitts. Patti, and Alvin were married three days after she turned 16 years old. They had three children: Alvin Joseph, Steven Louis, and Patricia Yvonne, commonly referred to as Angel.

Patti was in a high school choir right before her marriage. Whether the choir conductor wanted to encourage her to stay in school or for whatever reason, Patti understood her to say, "You will never be able to sing parts." Nothing could have been further from the truth! Patti later started her family Gospel group. They sang often at Wheeler Mission along with several other places around Indiana, travelling as far as Illinois. She also has sung with other Gospel groups, singing solos, to many people for over 50 years. Most enjoyable was her clowning for Jesus which she still does.

At the age of 23, Patti heard someone reading from the Bible, and it seemed to make more sense to her · than before. She then got up, walked up the stairs to her room, and told Jesus, with somewhat an indignant attitude, "Jesus, if You're real, let me know You better than I know anyone or anything else." Patti said she left that room a completely different person.

Near the time Patti was working for a sales advertisement paper, she became friends with Sandi and her daughter, Jessica, who happened to be one of her co-workers. Only too soon, she became aware that Jessica had tragically lost her son, Devon, after being run over by an automobile. Sandi (Mamaw), Jessica, and her sister, April, showed great faith in dealing with such a terrible loss. Patti then decided to write a poem to provide comfort for the family. Actually, the poem turned out to be long enough to become a short book. It is our hope that the poem you are about to read, Devon in Heaven will provide peace of mind to others, especially to those who have lost a child.

On February 16, 2002, Patti and I were married and along with AJ, Steve, Angel and my daughter, America, we became a bigger and happier family.

Ronald Newnum

Printed in the United States
By Bookmasters